Untumbled Gem

Poems

by

Julie A. Dickson

Julie A. Dickson

Goldfish Press

Seattle, Washington

ISBN 10: 0692717870
ISBN 13: 978-0692717875

Library of Congress Catalog Card Number 2016942292

For Dan

Julie A. Dickson

Untumbled Gem

Sometimes I am rough like an untumbled gem,

true essence hidden below the uncut surface.

An outward façade covers my deep red garnet heart,

spiritual warmth gently held in balance.

When polished with sunlight, I might glow

in facets of brilliance like a rose quartz;

but don't be deceived by my reflection –

for healing takes time under soft reiki-touch.

While gazing into seemingly endless depths,

the crystal light of my topaz-brown eyes

holds something else, as yet undefined

that mirrors a struggle you may have shared.

Five Willows Literary Review 2016

Bring Your Guitar

Whither we wander
travelin' on a forest path
tall pine trees loom overhead
and there's no turning back

Infuse the day with gladness
hold my hand as we walk along
stop among the forest trees
bring your guitar, play me your song

In this protected wilderness
where sunlight glows and branches sway
a melody moves past your lips
the words you sing can light my way

Avocet Journal of Nature Poetry 2015

Julie A. Dickson

Sunrise in New York City

Beckoning the red dawn sky

O'er the roof tops eagles fly

Light the morning, comes the day

Affecting how I choose my way

Carriaged laughter, glasses tink

Passersby cause me to think

Hearing chatter, murmured voice

I'd leave the chaos, given choice

Would sunrise rural sky enhance

Beyond the city walls, by chance?

The buildings tall, block virtue's dream

Quiet hillside thoughts redeem

Untumbled Gem

In trepidation I may walk

Towards something new as people talk

Through the rooftops out to plains

Venture forth where sunrise reigns

Will this new dawn become that day?

Down cobbled streets I'll find my way

Five Willows Literary Review 2016

Julie A. Dickson

Morning on the Bay

Daybreak water, surface like glass
eels move in ripples, terns glide past.
Morning on the bay, tide rose
small craft's wake parting still reposes.
Concentric circles move away
as boats on moorings pitch and sway.
Gulls post sentinel, watch from rocks;
cormorants land and foul the docks
Fish break surface, cause birds to swarm;
cast out lines before day turns warm.
On the point – heron majestic,
stands predicting as a mystic.
Fishermen follow terns' display,
hoping their holds are filled today.

First Sip of Coffee

Languorous lax,
Lethargic of motion
Heavy eyes lidded,
Closed to commotion

Aroma envelops,
Sleepiness sated
Reticent richness,
Tiredness abated

Sensation insurgent,
Warmed with one swallow
Alertness returning,
More cups to follow

Julie A. Dickson

Early Morning

The wonderment
of the early morning hours,
its stillness in nature
I reveled in the quiet
attuned with the crisp chill in the air,
I pulled my collar up around my neck
and exhaled visibly
The sun crept up over the crest of the building,
its yellow-white brightness
causing me to squint slightly;
I turned toward the north
as a flock of geese flew,
seemingly overdue
in their southbound migration
toward warmer climate
The emerging sun bathed the morning
in potions of brilliance
Arcs of light caressed the sky
poems of great longing
spun their tales
in the essence of dawn

Beneath the Ice

Water rushes along the river bed beneath the ice

The force of sand and silt erodes and carries along with it

The dust of months, swirling sediment into a frenzy of froth

As river bottom creatures slumber in thick mudded earth

A myriad of life awakens slowly in the river beneath the ice

Turtles buried deep stretch long quiet necks to peer out

Translucent eggs cling to rocks, ready for spring hatching

Beneath the ice an air pocket allows a lethargic snake

To careen through crevasses, rocks and ice-chilled water

A chunk of ice breaks free and journeys down the river

Becoming smaller, bumping and colliding against rocks

As the air warms, life echoes and awakens beneath the ice

The Portsmouth Herald: Random Acts of Poetry 2014

Julie A. Dickson

Seasons Passed

Beneath the deadfall of autumn
moldering under the melted snow of winter
lay a single rusting brass key,
without fob or ring, just a key -
A copy, you could tell by the markings,
no description or brand name
to identify what the lone key might unlock.

Caught in a rake tine, it roughly scraped,
dragged from the brown-edged lawn onto
pavement, causing me to glance down
at the sound- I lifted the rake to my gloved hand.
Plucking the key loose, I dropped it into
the pocket of my denim jacket and resumed
gathering old wet leaves and decayed twigs
into a pile, a myriad of dull winter saturated debris,
forgotten leaves past the glory of vibrant reds.

The huge maple leaves lay in a sad heap, no memory
of brilliant gold; I listened to the raspy strokes
of the rake on the pavement's edge, uncovering
strange silhouetted shapes, staining the spring walk
in odd patterns, Rorschach-like on the cement canvas.
My hand went unconsciously to the key in my pocket,
the rake forgotten, remembering seasons passed.

Avocet Journal of Nature Poetry 2014
Kind of a Hurricane Press: Four Seasons Anthology 2015

She Calls forth the Spring

Come into view my lovely yellows

Like the sun beaming on majestic meadows

Your heads turned toward bountiful rays

Blooming jonquils and daffodils

Bring forth the smiling spring

Chase away the winter chills

Now I call for the royal-regalia

The standing ovation of sunlight and rain

Springtime begs for your beauty

Pervasive purples to meander

Crocus and iris of reawakening

Festoon the fields, lovely lavender

Julie A. Dickson

Finally pure whites shine in unison

Snowdrops wave goodbye to winter

Trilliums trill as trumpets raised

Rejoicing in the springtime dew

Bitter Crest, a reminder of snow

Forget-me-nots forge anew

Avocet Journal of Nature Poetry 2014

Rain

Expectedly damp, cold and dank
The alleys and courtyards stank
Of mildewed wood, piles of refuse
About the state of things, I muse
When suddenly the droplets fall
Rain, unbidden, drenching all
Moisture rolls, grimy streaks descend
Leaves held in gutters, wait to send
Sodden debris joins the floating
Mini-rivers, storm drain bloating
No umbrella, caught under eaves
Up with collar, tug on sleeves
The alley drip-dries, unconcerned
What becomes wet, no rain discerns
Aftermath – crowds resume, hurry
We'll be late, they often worry

The Poet's Touchstone 2013

Moose

Standing still three feet deep,
with river at low tide,
head dipped as he ripped
weeds, and then he chewed.
The town from each bank
viewed an unusual beast
enjoying his feast from the river.
But then they came along,
those from Fish and Game,
we all nodded and agreed
our young moose bore no blame.
He [the moose] was made to go,
tranquilized without much bellow,
taken far up north to graze,
hoisted, as we pondered -
is this the best way to raise a moose?

Five Willows Literary Review 2015
Poetry Quarterly 2015

Caterpillar of Yellow

Caterpillar of yellow, a debonair fellow
crawls as inchworm up thistle and vine
Prefers yellow hue, and if I was you
I'd tell him he's decked out quite fine

Stylin' I'd say, you'd best back away
and let him get on with his task
Interrupt nature; don't try to assuage here
he'll tell you his plan if you ask

Munching on flower, alone by the hour
blend in like a camouflaged bird
Once eaten his fill, he'll be stayin' until -
on his way with nary a word

What's that you claim, you know his true name?
Acronicta Americana in books
Such a fuzzy guy, soon after he'll fly
once in branches his cocoon is hooked

Then after a time, while attached to the vine
miraculous change to occur
Emerge as from cloth, a young dagger moth
spreading his wings, flies away in a blur

The Poet's Touchstone 2014

Julie A. Dickson

Voice to Past, Beware

Break from the darkness, cocoon cast aside
emerge in brilliance, let your heart decide
spread your new winged majesty,
no more will you hide

The branch that held your prison cell collapsed
no more exists the smoth'ring arms that grasped
when you broke free from chrysalis,
the waiting tide elapsed

Unfurl the wings from dampness to the air
see the sun-bathed meadows, bending ferns fair
when flight from discarded captive state
has given voice to past, beware

I May Fly

Upon the yellow gentle flower
dainty steps of caterpillar,
sways the stem as he ambles
on his way to delicate leaves.
Hopelessly hungry,
on the green pungent branches
he moves along his way
and hesitates as bird flies by.
Hoping he is camouflaged,
his brightly striped body
enveloped by a garden rainbow.
I am not here; he projects in thought -
I am the flowers and the leaves.
Go on your way. Leave me to my meal.
My time is now, for soon I must sleep
and then I may fly, as you do.

Poetry Quarterly 2016

Butterfly

Atop an arc of gold
Nestled among
Snowy petals

The translucent nature of
Your wings is not unlike
A window pane

Look out on your world
Feel caress of breeze, sip
The sweet nectar

And fly away gracefully
Flutter to land on the next
Fragrant flower

Untumbled Gem

Emergence

A tightly coiled spring

compression in form,

helical twister

preluding a storm

A vernal deluge

bud springs from its womb

Equinoxical

emergence in bloom

Curled effervesced bud

bends toward the warm sun,

torsion unfolding;

signs - Spring has begun

Five Willows Literary Review 2016

Wet

Steady dripping, rain drips off wet branches,
patters, rhymic tapping on my forehead.

I close my eyes, can still see the droplets,
collecting in volume until they fall, in clear bulbous
splashes, like a hanging sack of water.

An erratic heartbeat as rain pummels,
soaking clothes and skin, washing away will.
Dark, swirling rivulets run together
downhill into deep inviting puddles.

Umbrellas cover heads, dripping water
dancing - a perverse ballet on shoulders,
saturated shoes squish on the pavement.

Voluminous clouds billow and cover
my wishful thoughts of a dry sunny day.

The Harvard Press 2014

Morning Pond

Silver glimmers through the haze,
morning dew and shadows fade
A bird, majestic sits on frond
as morning dawns upon the pond,
crickets chirp and frogs chime in,
without a care, the bird begins
to fish, unfettered by the day
Among the marshes, reeds and clay,
Heron seeing cormorant,
competing yet they do not daunt
the wildlife, nor other bird;
they jabber, some don't speak a word
of protest, there are fish for all
in the distance, loons that call
Egret, swoops and eats her catch
settles on a rock to watch
cousins feeding on the pond
white and silver, hear the sound

Smoky Quartz 2014
The Harvard Press 2014
Avocet Journal of Nature Poetry 2014

Julie A. Dickson

Mist

Swirled dancer's pale feet pirouette
Lightly brushing the pond surface.
Morning dew, a ballet performed
Filmy iridescent motion
Flowing over, while trees bow with
Graceful arms waving their farewell
To the fleeing ebony night,
Ushering in the sunrise – air
Kissing water, causing ripples
Lowing hanging fog dances across.
It swells and billows out like white
Drying sheets on a clothes-pinned line.
Morning calm broken only by
Startled windy gusts, sending mist
West to East toward a grassy knoll.
Small rodent in 2-legged stance
Peers over the gauzy-veiled pond,
Nourished by nature's dawn embrace;
Earth and air joined in a handshake
Liaison of early morning.

Avocet Journal of Nature Poetry 2013

Walk Away

Wrenching sadness, pulled through a gaping wound -
self-inflicted, but how else might one heal from a loss?
Once exposed to light, the thing might just fade away,
whither from lack of gloom, the dark whispers of grief.
One might notice a curling of edges, a subtle graying
on the former blood-red, crimson scar – yes
it's a start, a new beginning if you can take a chance,
walk away from abysmal fortitude - embrace anew.

Julie A. Dickson

Melt into Rhyme

When you allege an untruth,
attempt to drive a wedge -
I find it uncouth,
this type of descent
into the abyss of strife.

I would be remiss
if I failed to make good
or henceforth unveiled
the plans I understood
long ago we set forth.

We vowed to forego words,
allowed, written in pen -
at the time I was smitten,
unto you felt sublime,
caused me to melt into rhyme.

Five Willows Literary Review 2015

No Wry Attempt

When I find it difficult to relate
the need to placate when tempers are high,
no wry attempt to belie or abate -
I often tempt fate, elsewise imply;
However, refuse to lie or debate;
I prefer to create, or simply vie
without meaning to pry, or sound opaque -
can hardly sate my desire to fly.

Majestic Oak [for Rob]

Your spirit called,
in pain, despair
I answered you
hush, I am here

The herbs are cast
upon the wind;
release your pain
in darkness find

Your path to me,
I lead the way;
I stand before
you; come, I say

Follow me
my old oak friend;
sail with me
as your life ends

Majestic oak,
your soul to me;
I praise the stars
and set you free

Owl Speak [for Rob]

When an owl speaks your name, the end is near
On this point the Native beliefs are clear
Was your sketch of owl a premonition,
or in some silent way a prediction?

We might have known a talent such as yours
might be called too soon to leave our shores
Myriad voices call, were left behind
memories of choices serve to remind

Ageless friendship whispers your artful sound
and in owl's call is echoed from beyond.

Prey Tell 2015

A Hawk

I walk the rocky foothills through scrub pine;

above me hawk in lazy circle soars,

repeating pattern of some grand design,

Hawk spies a fish below as river pours

o'r stones and pebbles, loose as branches flow;

tangled, catch, break free, downstream they travel.

Held tight in talons, the hawk's prey in tow -

Has stirred up silt, swirls among the gravel.

Echoed sound of footsteps, path traversed,

he, solitary as my stride, the hawk.

I wander through existence well-rehearsed;

tranquility must feed me as I walk.

I feel the morning sun upon my face,

feel nurtured as within my love's embrace.

Prey Tell 2015

Hawk Eyes

In the meadow a bird flew
Over the snow white field
Precariously balanced
'Tween life and death
The gentle existence of time
Making the available morsel
Challenging and rarely found
When the constant hunger beckoned
Lonely in flight, he hung low in the air
Hawk eyes sharp on the ground
Detecting small movements below
Suddenly he dropped with claws outstretched
But, alas his prey escaped quickly
Into safe abode; tiny heart trembling,
In her mind she knew it could have been the hawk
Who feasted that day, instead of her,
Safe with winter stores below

Avocet Journal of Nature Poetry 2014
Prey Tell 2015

Julie A. Dickson

Hunger

Rust-toned wings of Kestrel flight
swoops down from cliff at morning light.
Her call permeates the air
as a minstrel strolls the fair.
Lizards, mice run from her path,
she soars down but bears no wrath.
Simple hunger, ancestral drive
carries in talons, her prey alive.
Over grasslands, buoyant flight
lands on cliffs just out of sight
Boisterous boast on high, her tell-
screeches to the wind, Kestrel.

Prey Tell 2015

Citadel against Time

Watching the night sky, I see owl at last
long to be creative, words to be cast.
They dwell within, a stronghold is my mind
I am as stone, citadel against time.

The sky streaked blue-gray in the pre-dawn night,
Barred Owl mournful at the emerging daylight.
His parting calls are all sharply uttered,
as escaping phrases, mind less cluttered.

The departing owl, wings off toward the wood
sunrise approaches, I'd sing if I could,
my farewell – night raptor leaves the skyline,
I'm still as stone, citadel against time.

Prey Tell 2015

Julie A. Dickson

Healing Wings

The waves of pain struck at my heart like daggers

Unseen forces against a mighty fortress, battered

Crumbled with age, gradual wearing away

Time knew no healing to the damage inflicted upon me

The storm kept on, icy wind chilled me to the bone

The hood of my jacket offered little protection

And thunder rolled in the distance, as if in warning

My soul cried out to no one, my anguish knew no end

My eyes closed, heart ached; overhead a cry was heard

A lone eagle answered the question of my heart, why?

He answered wordlessly, all knowing and wise

A huge span of wings, his stark unfriendly eyes

Yet he knew my pain and anguish, like no one could

He defined me in seconds, where man had failed

The shriek of the eagle sang to my sadness as I gazed

Hand shielding my eyes, a slight smile came to my lips

He flew gracefully away, his message to me echoing

I felt nourished by his solitude, my pain felt numbed

If only for a moment, I knew I shared his glory of flight

The healing of his wings fluttered against my heart.

Julie A. Dickson

The Spirit of the Rock

Overhead the shrill cry
of the hawk pierces my head;
look up as the sun blinds me
I can only hear his voice,
but my vision is distorted
by the sheer rock above me

Broken rock crystals fall
into deep crevices below,
ring into my ears until
the pounding shards
cease their echo,
into the dampened earth below

The beads of sweat trickle
down my neck unnoticed,
my hold on the rock
ceaseless
I pause to let my mind drift
into the largeness of time

As I feel there
before me
the looming stone,
face of eternity,
and the insignificant
being I am

Standing closely,
Aware, and
one constant thought
threatens my peace of mind;
but no thoughts allowed when
held by the spirit of the rock

The Poet's Touchstone 2011

Known by Many Names

Gaia speaks as Mother Earth, whispers softly to her child

Child answers Isis, goddess of trees and forests wild

Pachamama swaddles babe and holds him to her breast

Babe at the vast hillside, snuggles Demeter's ample chest

Nokomis feeds a bounty, daughter of the moon abides

Longs for Earth sustainable, Jord the mother, life provides

Danu nurtures fauna, she walks upon majestic plains

Call we must to Maka, Earth Mother known by many names

Anu hangs her head dismayed, a sadness wells up in her soul

Children cease to honor earth, wilderness since times of old

Mother Nature, Goddess weeps a flood eternally

Feels the loss of nature, the Earth not what it's meant to be

Five Willows Literary Review 2014
Avocet Journal of Nature Poetry 2014

Julie A. Dickson

Echoes of Conscience

Ask the important questions in silence
Perhaps you'll hear the echoes of conscience

Resistance to responsibility
May be the proof of mediocrity

When given right to freedom, it's taken
Is accountability forsaken?

Clever intellectuals might converse
Humanity won't function in reverse

Destruction, ruin, well-documented
While peaks of accomplishments are mounted

If all mankind stayed settled on the ground
He might find the answers that must be found

Is there time to forge a path to repair
Or are humans destined to disappear?

Avocet Journal of Nature Poetry 2015

Peacemaker

Who can be the peacemaker
Keeping us content,
Calming all our differences
With harmonious intent?

Who can solve all crises
And end the lasting struggle,
Preserving calm tranquility
Preventing future trouble?

Is there such a person
For I would come to know,
That with her mere existence
A peaceful calm would grow

People in agreement
Disputes forever waned,
Knowing that hostilities
Would not be seen again

Truly, we must wonder
If quarrels can ever end
Can we be the peacemakers
With the means to send

Our message to all people
To seek and find a way
To communicate and listen,
And find peace, day by day

The Poet's Touchstone 2011

Julie A. Dickson

A Feather [mirror poem]

On this, a day of perfect weather,
Against the pale blue sky - a feather
Streak of white as clouds pass by,
Appears as sketched from artist's eye
After which the canvas clears
When in the noonday sky appears,
Imaginary shapes portray
A moving picture, vast array
As if to entertain and show
The world – a ceaseless, timeless flow
                ~ ~ ~
The world – a ceaseless, timeless flow
As if to entertain and show
A moving picture, vast array
Imaginary shapes portray
When in the noonday sky appears,
After which the canvas clears
Appears as sketched from artist's eye
Streak of white as clouds pass by,
Against the pale blue sky - a feather
On this, a day of perfect weather

The Harvard Press 2014
Five Willows Literary Review 2014
Avocet Journal of Nature Poetry 2014

Pomaceous

Pomaceous Orbs glisten with dew

in the morning sun, succulent morsels

shine yellow-red behind translucent leaves.

The clusters nestled in gnarled tree forks,

weigh down slender sapling branches

awaiting the eager hands of harvest.

Gather them now into your basket.

Drink in their aroma, coolly crisp;

savory apple, each snap in your mouth.

Five Willows Literary Review 2015

Julie A. Dickson

Oasis of Land

When I first met you it was on an island.

Waves lapped at the rocks, but I didn't notice.

Your face reflected every sunny day in my life,

your voice a rainbow of tones, both high and low.

The wind may have blown that day, I don't recall.

I saw your eyes, as blue as the sky and your hand

cupped over your brow as we spoke.

Gulls may have screamed and swooped overhead.

But I felt only the two of us on that island -

though birds and the ocean surrounded us.

Star Island, an oasis of land – a creative space,

light house bell echoing like a heartbeat.

Avocet Journal of Nature Poetry 2016

Window Tells a Story

Mem'ries told for each tomorrow,
tales recalled of yesteryear.
a gentle breath with every ocean swell -
window has a story to tell.

Footfalls echo, wooden treads,
faded opalescent threads
most people here will only see the view,
softened light through fabric frame,
sunset fading like a candle flame.

The window won't reveal who
it will tell its story to…

Mem'ries told for each tomorrow,
tales recalled of yesteryear,
a gentle breath with every ocean swell -
window has a story to tell.

Peering through translucent lens,
curtain billows, dark descends;
passing visions etched onto the sky.
Stand upon the ancient stair
listen for the window to share.
The window won't reveal who
it will tell its story to…

Julie A. Dickson

The window won't reveal who
[Maybe it will be for you...]

Mem'ries told for each tomorrow,
tales recalled of yesteryear,
a gentle breath with every ocean swell -
window has a story to tell.

[Co-written with Dan Miner 2014]

Ripples

Swirling mists
Upon the walk
In silence
Through the fog
The vast expanding
Quiet sea
In ripples
Blowing endlessly

Avocet Journal of Nature Poetry 2013

Julie A. Dickson

One Last Night

Do roses in ruin shine by the moon
on one last night, make a brave stand,
Withered petals dripping with dew?
Do the petals fail to fall when caressed by
moonlight, exclaimed essence ebbing away?

When morning dawns do their heads droop
with a fated sorrowful fragility?
Do they sense their eventual end?

Sunflowers [Van Gogh- Ekphrasis]

Happy sunflower faces gathered
with the most boisterous standing tall
as part of a diverse family, leaders apparent,
they call out for notice.
One with wide eyes, an owl's piercing stare upon its
surroundings, surveying, guarding offspring
with sharp talons to protect from perceived foes

Others, partially hidden, like a shy squirrel
camouflaged behind trees
hoping not for notice, but to be invisible
among woodland shadows.
Many stand shorter than exuberant siblings –
do not speak out but they hear.

And one whose face studies the ground,
an undernourished kid, a wraith
hoping as the runt of his litter to find
enough food and sunlight to survive

Sunflowers stand together - the bold,
the sisters with lithe beauty, the hidden,
the sick and dying, until their faded golden petals
are dispersed to the wind

Avocet Journal of Nature Poetry 2013

Julie A. Dickson

Humming

A low-pitched drone reverberates
the hollow tree like a bass symphony.
Wing-ed conductors move about in the air,
the bark is alive and crawling with life
as the swarm mimics a thick blanket.

Humming in a unison concerto,
laboriously for their shared task,
as scouts fly reconnaissance, returning
heavy with nectar to blend with the masses.

They seem to signal others to depart;
the queen surveys her realm from
a protected inner sanctum – all work
performed skillfully, without complaint.

The Poet's Touchstone 2014
The Harvard Press 2015

Foot Down

Crimson ball hangs low in the sunset sky
dances brightly on burning hot car hood.
A wind-blown scarf flies away from my neck,
whipping erratically against my face.

Desert scrub brush is mirrored, reflected
in shiny hubcaps, highway markers blurred.
Eyes try to focus - the monotonous,
long stretch of road, faux oasis beckons;
my throat grows thick with thirst, its silent scream
for water permeates every thought.

I'm not wandering on the desert floor
but speeding, with top down, my eyes burning
in tinted lenses, car red as scarlet
sun, foot down racing to the horizon.

Avocet Journal of Nature Poetry 2015

The Choice

Caught between two worlds, no answers can be found
Voice echoes in confusion; I lie prone upon the ground
The force great and mighty calls from far away
To urge me ever onward, though I'm caught up in the fray

The darkness is compelling; it's driven me from pain
In shadows, hidden heartache; in silence felt the strain
Give in to dark abysmal night, weary bones to rest
Just close my eyes to sunrise, let silence fill its quest

In one, the world opens; a new path shows itself to me
A hand extends to lead the way, the future and my destiny
The other, ever silent, gloomy shadows call my name
Still, the release from vast unrest, I seek to end the game

With the will of fortitude, the forces clash to make me blind
But in eternal platitude, the choices clear within my mind
I stand and walk now toward you, I clasp the outstretched hands
The darkness far behind me, the will of life commands

Page & Spine 2013

Stop Time

When you hear the music play,
But only for awhile
Let the forces carry you,
Allowing just a smile

Echoed voices answer
Tomorrow's dreams are mine,
Yesterday is fading
The traces all unwind

Wander through the courtyard
Hear the silence wane
Faces mirror sadness,
The suffering to claim

To wake in your arms
Remembering the kiss
Once I am alone again,
Is something that I miss

To hold you so close,
To feel your heart pound
To lie in your arms
And not make a sound

To dwell in your warmth,
Your arms touching mine
And just for awhile,
I'd like to stop time

hunger [triolet]

hunger is a lonely child
longing for acceptance
searching life in forces wild
hunger is a lonely child

remembered kindness when she smiled
approved your acquiescence
hunger is a lonely child
longing for acceptance

Touch Nothing

Is it better to touch cold stone than to touch nothing?

You might recognize my language, my protective mode,

like the familiar backing away

of a fleeting shadowed figure,

the last remnant of a dream fragment upon waking.

My dreams are like characters in a novel, they walk

across my heart, leaving their footprints.

Is it better to let go of emptiness, to feel even pain?

Shall I fill my empty heart, my open palm with cool water,

To sample life's nectar, or is it better to touch nothing,

and to let nothing touch me?

Five Willows Literary Review 2016

Julie A. Dickson

Angels Dancing

In her eyes he saw angels dancing;
She was dreamlike in her motions.
Her manner appeared carefree
yet he knew she was guarded.
She had a heart, of that he was sure,
but it lay crushed and broken
among shards of glass and rubble.
He could see pain in her eyes
and he longed to hold her,
whisper reassuring words.
He wanted her to smile,
for him to be the reason why.
In her voice he heard music
Melodies of hope and songs of love
emerging from her lips.
He wanted to share the music with her,
to be the cause of her singing.
He gazed into her eyes and
saw angels dancing there.

Forest Nectars 1997
Van Gogh's Ear 2014

No Reply

Starscaped darkness
When in flight
Lights of brightness
Day to night

Drift away
From wayward thought
Where in lifetime
Dreams are naught

Catch the drifting
Clouds 'cross sky
Lying back
The thoughts are neigh

Shadows reflect
In empty space
With the vast
And hollow place

Echoed emptiness
Prevailed
Attempts at contact
All have failed

Where within
My heart does lie
I hear no answer,
No reply

Julie A. Dickson

Stars

Lay back and rise above
to see the stars,
dare to escape the perils of day,
to be with darkness
with the points of light,
suggesting worlds beyond

Imagine a world of unknown life,
stars as the velvet cloth of sky
that blankets the earth,
bathes the quiet nighttime,
while you gaze above
and whisper to no one

Avocet Journal of Nature Poetry 2014

Birdsong

The last spoken word
Lost on a breeze
Forsaken, mistaken
Two wrens in the trees

Sweet birdsong repeated
Echoed through the cool air
They're sated, elated
The wren's song rang clear

The nest was entwined
Grasses woven and wound
With instinct, succinct
The hatchings were bound

On opposite branches
Wrens perched in the wood
Protected, deflected
Watching over their brood

Today nest is vacant
Hatchlings, wrens are gone
sky clear, they disappear
I'll miss their birdsong

The Poet's Touchstone 2014
Avocet Journal of Nature Poetry 2014

Julie A. Dickson

Premonition

I may have held my breath

during a hot day in late August,

almost angry to see a red leaf so soon,

as if its mere presence shocked me,

the premonition mounting like a crescendo

The curtain of season-change drops,

warmth fading, seemingly in just one day –

caught, the red, a stray blown leaf,

lost, while others rejoice, sharing their brilliance.

Avocet Journal of Nature Poetry 2015

Trees Aflame [Triolet]

Autumn set the trees aflame
Nature does as she will please
Don't blame night, it's not to blame
Autumn set the trees aflame

Blaze of color is her claim
Turns the gold and crimson leaves
Autumn set the trees aflame
Nature does as she will please

Avocet Journal of Nature Poetry 2014

Mums the Word

Autumn arrives in russet regalia

and mums the word on every front porch.

Euro Pink like a dazzling Azalea,

Sunny Morn Yellow a blazing bright torch.

The fortitude of Fuchsia Spider Mums

Rorschach shapes loom shadows on garden walk.

Drink of Red Gypsy Wine when evening comes,

Court Jester dances as if he could talk.

Poetry Quarterly 2016

Crimson Spire

Tall oak reaches like a spire of green
against blue expansive sky I've seen;
crowded branches slowly sway
transform to Crimson Spire by day.

Nearby maple, Autumn Flame
beckoning change, fulfills its name
as if painted by an artist's brush,
first at branch ends, gently touch.

When forest green decides to purge,
struck with a vermillion urge,
during cool mornings instead discover
shades of russet one after another.

Some gilded-golds aspire to compete -
Crimson Spire's life span is bittersweet.
Even Autumn Flame will fade to brown
while a palette of red leaves tumbles down.

Avocet Journal of Nature Poetry 2014

Acorn

I thought I recognized
A gnarled oak upon this path
My eyes search the tree line
Perhaps I am mistaken
Acorns at my feet roll
Among roots and brush
I hear a far-off cry
A lone red-tailed hawk
Gliding lazily above
Reminding me of something
Just beyond the edge of thought
The outcropping of rock ahead
Stands as sentry to beyond
I pause to pay homage to stone and sky
In this ancient forest I walk
As others may have in past lives,
No remnant of voices reach my ears
I am but an acorn in this quiet forest
But for the hawk's cry
Warning or beckoning
Causing me to glance up
Shielding my eyes from brightness,
His shadowed form casts shadows
On the ground, and on my doubts
Banishing them into the abyss
Like pebbles thrown down
A sacred stone well

The Harvard Press 2016

On Its Way to Somewhere

Wave ripple down as sparkling diamonds
Over rocks as they splash and fall
The gentle whisper of stream is pleasant
My ears behold the sound as I sit
Contemplating the sky
As the clear blueness reaches out
Like fine cloth covering my head
The blanket above the tree line
Blue against green,
Small branches disappearing into sky
From this distance I can only see
The largeness of trunks and the blur of leaves
Hiding invisible life within safe branches
The birds dwell in nest, a squirrel or spider
But from far away, life may not exist
Only that I know it is there, hidden from view
Restless is a blowing leaf
Across the burnt out land
Catching in a crack and
Breaking free to fly again
Unsettled, cannot light for long
Traveling through the sky as though
Searching outward purposefully
Must find the way to fly alone
Flies along, past leaf-filled trees
Not recognizing allies there
Not joining familiarity
Just well on its way to somewhere

Bully's Façade

Irrepressible vestige of sorrow

with solemn audible sighs

is one you'd be wise not to borrow.

You prefer an august fortitude

with justifications balanced,

anyone listening might conclude.

You are adept in your disguise

but underneath a thin veneer,

the façade you've learned to improvise,

Veiled exterior, feigned arrogance

surrounds your vulnerability;

your chosen protection is not by chance.

Bullied into Silence 2014

She Cries

Hair like strands of hay escaping a bale
found in a scrawny pale blond pony tail
I think about this briefly- they compare,
discussing this lovely girl's flaxen hair

And a small equine's fine tail adornment-
merely to add additional torment,
prod and tease, then coax her until she cries;
the young girl's fragile tears fall and he tries

To convince her that she would be unloved
though she might choose to wish on stars above;
don't be concerned about her loving you,
a hurtful boy, who could not know love- true

We sit in silence and I hold her hand,
assuring her that I can understand.
Harsh words are spoken for effect, no gain
bullying is not all physical pain.

Bullied into Silence 2014

Julie A. Dickson

Big Boys

Facedown in a snow bank,
my brother lay frozen and still
not wanting to incite more anger
from the kids that attacked him;
though what he did to deserve
a torn jacket and a face full of snow,
he would never find out.

I stood far away, afraid to move
until the big boys wandered off,
until their laughter died down
as they rounded the corner
on their way to buy candy at the store;
as if the most natural sequence of events
was to tear my brother's jacket and push him
face first into snow and then buy candy.

Bullied into Silence 2014

Touching Stone

Cold, the cool marble – hard as ice

but as ice melts upon your touch, the stone does not.

The silent lack of echo – the faceless marble waits.

When your hand reaches out to touch, it bites [the cold].

Smooth as glass – but no reflection emitted,

its inner nature remains a secret to probing eyes.

Rough, a granite textured rock

granular and speckled like a bird's egg.

Unlike a fragile eggshell, granite endures

against time, unbroken unless from man;

carefully hewn and shaped, or

gouged by water's force, persistent.

You watch, touching stone.

As a rock, I stand in time.

Avocet Journal of Nature Poetry 2016

Julie A. Dickson

Lucius

He carried a bronze, hand carved caduceus.

His long robes billowed and swayed as he walked,

though none dared utter, his name was Lucius;

the people stood in stark fear when he talked.

His fierce some staff was far worse than a sword;

Lucius- the nobles, he held in suspense.

The power he wielded brought him reward;

from kings and bishops, he sought recompense.

In dismay the monarchs plotted revenge,

the serfdom was searched, through village and town.

The king sought a champion, brave to avenge;

in secret, the plot was to bring Lucius down.

By morning the king felt relief, plan deployed.

Throughout the kingdom they heard Lucius' cries.

In crux of passion caduceus destroyed;

the truth- a fair maiden caused Lucius' demise.

Dance like the Fire

Dance like the fire above a candle wick
Floating free, arms sway in gentle rhythm
Amber and vermilion glow as flames lick
Music synchronized as beats from a drum

Garments of silk and gauze swirl around
Your legs while you twirl and turn fluidly
Sparks illuminate night enhance the sound
Voices harmonize, join in fiery plea

Hands held high above as if they might see
Look up to the night sky in reverie

The Poet's Touchstone 2015

Julie A. Dickson

She Stands Alone

Down to the rolling azure sea she walks
while waves dance and lap at the rocky shore.
I watched her leave and what worries me more,
every song she sings and the way she talks.

The echoed phrases as she cries out loud,
her screams blending with gulls overhead,
her poor tortured face, her heart filled with dread,
her pale eyes veiled as if beneath a shroud.

I long to gather her frail body close,
to heal the damaged soul as we gaze -
lost in the motion, pain washed out on waves,
sheltered in warmth despite cold wind that blows.

Instead, she stands alone, but not so brave;
the chance I once had to join her had passed,
resigned I walk away from her at last,
as I realize her soul I can't save.

Nature's Metaphors

On rock strewn banks of Lapis Lazuli
lovely lavender catmint blossoms full
while the birds fly over sing *Claire de Lune*,
a *Faberge*-egg of porcelain lies,
single white stone upon the water's edge;
with sparkling waves lapping at Emerald Isles.
Mangrove trees standing tall at attention
surrounded by the fragrant voice of dew.
Dew drops fall on pliable branches, bow -
leaning over as lithe graceful dancers
set in curtsy before a waltz begins.
The light in opulent brilliant water
mirrored chestnut brown irises gaze on;
lashed perfectly, dark curtains shading,
shrouding warm expressive eyes- echoing.
A low braying welcomes Morning Glories,
the ruby breasted robin steps lively
over trembling tall grasses- lilies dance
on dainty feet wearing Lady Slippers.
Prince o' Pine finely dressed bows serenely
honoring Queen Anne's lace, her divine dance.
Delicate cotton-tipped Pussy Willows
stand as guards over Jack in the Pulpit-
he beckons worship from woodland masses.
Quiet audience of green moss and fern
among the whispering willow branches
caress the air and seem not to listen
to royalty of Purple Finch, contrasts
muted brown of Sparrow and Chickadees.

A spotted fawn grazing aside her doe;
boulders as ivory shoulders worn so smooth
by relentless deep azure waves and tide;
ebony echoes of reeds and thistle
swaying in a unison sidestep and
recall memories of Forget-Me-Nots;
brilliant bouquets burst in colorful hues,
bless-ed nature's chorus of harmony.

Julie A. Dickson

Gargoyles

Stone creatures stand their posts,
gargoyles against the night -
protecting helpless people who
dwell within their fortress.

Their feelings hidden,
unshown to any who enter;
strong faces without questions,
deaf ears turned outward.

Against the cruel voices,
unseeing eyes against
the world of ugliness;
they cannot speak.

No harm to the soul,
even though the thoughts
within the walls are held,
emotions lay deep within.

Dreams are held against hope;
nothing penetrates the walls;
the stone creatures
would never allow it.

Forest Nectars 1997

.

Mulled Over

I sit on the old porch swing,

roughened wood and frayed ropes

moving slowly with a creaky sway;

smoke curling from a heavy mug

of hot steaming mulled wine.

Rocking, I am transported back -

memories rustle like dry leaves

pulling at the outer fringes,

an elusive fragrance I crave,

tugging and teasing at my senses.

Visions of you distorted by tears,

no sounds of laughter present now;

your touch empty from my hand.

Mulled aroma of cloves envelops me;

only cinnamon and dreams remain.

Kind of a Hurricane Press: Nalpalm & Novacaine 2015

Julie A. Dickson

Colored Silk

Shreds of colored silk fly
as birds streak on magic wings;
images of red and blue
dance across my eyes.

Where is my solace
but in colorful sky,
peaceful in the rose of sunset,
faded blues in white expanse?

I gaze off into daylight,
eyes centered on cloud filled sky,
dreaming of tomorrows
when colors might touch me.

Avocet Journal of Nature Poetry 2014

First on the Scene

Over the crest of a hill, I drove -
first glimpse through a fog-veiled light beam,
headlights illuminating a field of diamonds,
glittering the bejeweled roadway, but no…

My approach revealed broken glass, strewn,
cut-edged shatters reflecting the light.
High beams joining the moonlit sky
across a mostly barren landscape
and beyond the sea of broken glass – a car.
Transfixed, slowing almost to a stop,
my eyes moved suddenly to the tire.
How obscure, the vision straight ahead,
a spinning tire thrust into the air.

Escaping my lips, an abrupt sound, incredulous
as my mind began to grasp this scene.
The initial imagined beauty, crystalline
shimmers against the dark highway
fell away like a fading smile.

Julie A. Dickson

A twisted hulk lay diagonally across my lane;

feeling a black foreboding welling up -

I parked, sensing the unfolding nightmare.

Was I asleep?

All night driving, an endless journey

etched into my thoughts like a deep chasm.

Engine finally quiet, I opened the door

and emerged into the night, listening.

A sharp sound forced my head to turn

to a lone tree by the road; I squinted to see

a wide-eyed sentinel, silhouetted against the sky.

The owl sent a mournful message.

The scene opened silently before me;

I stood unmoving, taking in the macabre.

Seconds passed as hours, powerlessness

to move or to react, I finally called out.

Hearing only the echo of my own voice,

eyes fell again on the owl, who stared,

a perceived messenger of death.

Five Willows Literary Review 2016
Kind of a Hurricane Press: Shattered 2016

Snow Sky

The whiteness of sky
Before the snow falls
Heavy air hangs overhead
Something impending as though
Waiting for guests to arrive
Their white lace and finery,
Pressed cotton cloth
Crisply pleated and worn,
I look up to dream-like white,
Remember skies of other days
When clear sun beckoned me
For now, the snow prevails,
Masking the warmth of sun

Avocet Journal of Nature Poetry 2015

Julie A. Dickson

I'd Never Make You Cry

If I were a man, I'd wear a felted hat,

walking tall down the dark street,

a knowing glance to those I meet.

If I were a man, I'd have my arm around your shoulder,

proud to be seen with you,

a treasure, come real and true.

If I were a man, I'd never make you cry.

I'd recognize your strengths and good,

revel in your worth, I would.

But I'm not a man, I don't know what it's like

to walk in your shoes -

even if I could choose,

I'd never make you cry.

Five Willows Literary Review 2015
Poetry Quarterly 2015

Wearing Mother's Shoes [Pantoum]

When you're wearing mother's shoes
The heels make high-pitched tapping sounds
Mother always looks amused
When daughter wears her costly gowns

The heels make high-pitched tapping sounds
Clomping 'cross the kitchen floor
When daughter wears her costly gowns
Dressed in pearls from dresser drawer

Clomping 'cross the kitchen floor
Mother always looks amused
Dressed in pearls from dresser drawer
When you're wearing mother's shoes

The Poet's Touchstone 2015

Julie A. Dickson

What Did We Do To You?

What did we do to you we cry,
as many brothers and sisters die

Our family pods just glide along
as rhythmically as a well-known song

You swim in our sea, we watch you learn;
humans are strange but we do not turn

Away from you, we often stay,
and near your boats, you watch us play

Among the waves, we glide, we sail,
propelled along by our strong tails

Not all of you are bad we know,
we've even helped you far below

When dangers threatened human life,
dolphins rescued you from strife

And still you pay us back this way,
humans now see us as prey?

The ocean is no place for you;
we live out in the sea that's blue

We cannot teach our kind to flee
from our home beneath the sea

We cannot visit you on land,
better you stay upon your sand

Dolphins were too trusting, true
but what did we ever do to you?

Elephants in Sanctuary

Old leathery façade all but hid the warm hearts,
swaying in unison, the gray pair stood touching,
almost embracing, two old elephants -
trunks intermittently entwined, reassured each other.

Ears alert, waving off small gnats that pester
ankles scarred from the memory of chains not forgotten,
years to trust the creatures that only confused,
bringing food and hay, yet also pain of hook and sticks,
uncertainly waiting in fear, dignity all but vanquished.

Their majesty of size was no help to them then;
they were larger but were diminished into
loneliness and solitude.

Those scars served to remind of long years captive, alone.
In the vast depths of their souls, they suffered,
enduring the cruelness of those they had trusted -
beaten when unhappy, for defending their pride.

The long wait for rescue, final sanctuary in old age,
now in solitude, the freedom painfully earned -
beneath the sun, among trees and grass,
lying down in deliciously muddy ponds,
swaying in unison, the elephant friends
will remember the past together.

Julie A. Dickson

Instincts

Fly in perfect V formation
How they know their destination
With predetermined concentration,
Geese fly

A quest their longer sense of time
The gray beasts follow from behind
Continue in a single line
Elephants return

The current harsh but swim they may
Orange flashing bodies flip in spray
Jump and propel, they know the way
Salmon spawn

Animals with their instincts known,
Purpose clear, many beasts have shown
Watch, listen, scent as wind has blown,
Animals know

Humans can't seem to comprehend
Instead they seek out land - defend
Power sought, from the foes they fend
Man's folly

The Harvard Press 2014
Avocet Journal of Nature Poetry 2015

Listen Closely

Whales, man to live together
Each in peace, free forever
To be brothers, not have to flee
Man as friend, not enemy

Heart are heavy, the sea belongs
To those who live there, wild and strong
Ancient creatures of the deep,
Teach to us the words to keep

Shrill laughter, peaceful calls
Whale's music fills the halls
Strong words, gentle, firm
Whales, man, each in turn

Sorrow, joy, whales call once more
And still they answer as before
Much to learn from seas below,
Listen closely, begin to grow

Massachusetts Cetacean Institute 1989
Avocet Journal of Nature Poetry 2015

Julie A. Dickson

Solitude

Where am I in solitude?
When do I release
my inward inhibitions
and create my inner peace

How do I discover
my motives and my truths,
my everyday existence,
my loneliness obtrused

If people see about me
the things I wish to hide;
I can only face myself
and put my fears aside

GFWC NH State Poetry Contest 1st place 1988
The Harvard Press 2014

Diminish the Emptiness

Organized your emptiness
In your mind revealed
The chaos overtakes you
Painful feelings sealed

Emptiness is filled with
Cluttered piles retained
Keeping them all detailed
Has left you feeling drained

Replace your heartache
With newly found dreams
Former existence
Is not what it seems

Choose your path wisely
Search for your soul
The chaos surrounds you
But can't make you whole

When questions can't be asked
And answers are not found
Diminish the emptiness
And leave without a sound

This Path

I recognize this path, I've walked before
Song drifts on air, it's sad; so like your voice
Along this path I sigh, recall once more
What might have been if I received a choice

No, I won't cry, refuse the threat of tears
Once hand in hand with you I wandered then
Cannot re-live the pain, so many years
My broken heart reminds me who I've been

Now I remember you with honest eyes
My trust was broken, tossed like so much dirt
You plunged a blade of words wrapped in your lies
But I refuse to dwell upon the hurt

Alone now, and although I might complain
I might decide to walk this path again

Ceaseless Chatter

Pedantic patter and ceaseless chatter
Plethora of propensity
Egotistic echoes, seek the shadows
Hides morose mediocrity

Within shrouded silence all was shattered
Quite calm, unusually unencumbered
Noticed all was gone that really mattered
Without all the useless blather

Uniquely undulated, thoughts absurd
Billowed in blustery winds that gust
Meaningless messages no longer heard
I cannot hear a single word

Julie A. Dickson

Hidden from View

Turn not from the face right in front of you
I can see just a trace, hidden from view
Time now echoes when you felt alone
You may not be used to love when it's shown

Tremulous mem'ries, the whispers of blame
No stranger's glances need make you feel shame
I can't recall when I started to feel
In darkness I wonder, chance that it's real

The journey short, you need not travel far
Set aside your fears; embrace who you are
Whenever chaos rules, just remember me
In my eyes you shine – who you're meant to be

Turn not from the face right in front of you
I can see just a trace, hidden from view

Crumbs

A stone hermitage hidden
By overgrown brambles,
thorny vines cast protection
barring the way of those
who wander the wrong path.
You ignore the posted sign
A caution against intruders.

You manage to part dense branches
enough to peer through thick shrubs
and glance at a filthy window,
a dim light shines from within
the building with a dark foreboding.

Scratches will mark your legs and arms
as you step across prickly threshold,
tiny insects will bother and bite
but they go unnoticed when you finally see
her face outlined from between drapery folds
Perhaps some would call you brave
as you proceed over broken flagstones,
recalling the wild gray hair in disarray,
gnarled old hands and her hunched back.

Your small hand grasps the tarnished knocker.
Standing quietly on the decaying porch,
you hear shuffled footsteps approach.
When the heavy oak door creaks open
an old woman stands before you;
a smile does not disclose your plan.

Julie A. Dickson

From your pocket a faded blue book,
your outstretched hand extends to hers -
a leather-bound book she takes right away,
her mouth in a mostly toothless grin.
You enter, smelling molasses cookies

Soft and warm from the old oven,
shared on a chipped china plate.
Sitting, she watches you wipe crumbs
from your face, her voice breathless as
she reads aloud from the blue volume

Poetry Quarterly 2015

Pattern

The pattern you weave
is one I know well,
working the loom
as I sit for a spell.

The pattern you knit
a double cable stitch
I love the sweater but
wool makes me itch.

The pattern you sew,
the dress I will wear,
all the fabrics you touch
with artistic flair.

The pattern I don
today walking in town;
come walk now beside me
and lay your work down.

Julie A. Dickson

She Walks

Shards of glass fell, not as silent tears,
lay in shadowed light below the door.
In the quiet aftermath she stands
back against the wall, her defense.

Waiting, listening in frozen stance
her glance beyond the closed door-
no longer captive; her hand reaches out
to turn the lock, glass crunches underfoot;
sanity remains tenuous at best.

Her footsteps meet the ground -
cautiously, over stones and roots;
her mind flashes to his raised hand,
wedding band glinting, almost blinding;
no longer will she listen to clever words,
spoken to justify anger – her fault?

Standing alone upon the path leading away
from the meek existence, forward to the unknown -
freedom beckoned previously but she could not hear.
Internal will finally shouts out clear and loud
to keep walking, feet upon path; she walks.

The Poet's Touchstone 2013

For Theo [brother of Vincent Van Gogh]

The sorrow runs deep, he stands alone
Aching in loss for the one he held dear
Standing up for the sanity of his brother,
Never knowing whether Vincent was sane

He defends his brother's life and work,
As if it could not stand alone
No one might appreciate the brilliance
If Theo were not to speak of it openly

Perhaps if they understood -
His reputation would not be tarnished,
Vincent's name would be protected
And sheltered with the love he craved

Perhaps they would regret their harsh words,
Spoken in cruelty and out of fear;
From what unkind words come from the lips
Of those who are not afraid?

Speak them, and deny their own madness,
Be it that he was insane, and not they
For those who would take pity on the mad,
Could be themselves considered mad

Still, poor Theo suffers on in silence,
His death just an echo of Vincent's unhappiness
An echo of pain, confusion and a wish to find
The peace and solitude the Vincent craved

Only in death is the work appreciated
And yet, what of the noble brother, whose words
Brought art's very existence to light?
Will he be forgotten?

Julie A. Dickson

Cruel ones, look inward to yourselves;
Honor the work, the pain and anguish
Art is conceived in passion, love and agony;
It is a process not without sacrifice

There are those who bear the gift
Of words, song, dance or the stage;
Bear in mind the visual splendor of the canvas,
Recorded in color, the soul of the artist
There is no greater gift an artist can give
Than to share his innermost thoughts and dreams
Captured by pen and ink, brought to life,
And hope that someone might understand

What is art, but a cry to be heard?
A hand reaching out, in color and design,
A statement of feeling, where words are few,
Will they know the meaning?

Five Willows Literary Review 2016

Your Video Friend

Silently, I stand waiting
Eyes straight forward, unblinking
Arms hanging idly at my sides

My coin-slot is at the ready
Affixed to post and gate
I take quarters, nickels, dimes

Awaiting lonely children
Who have no other friend
I stand until I'm needed

A lone figure approaches
Looks into my stolid face
Mesmerized and greeted

With the sign that boasts
I will be your video friend
Insert coins to play with me

I hear the quarters drop
And then the metal click
For this child I am free

My eyes blink, my arms move
I take a step from the post
A small hand grasps mine

We walk and play and talk
A child's smile is my reward
I wish we had more time

Julie A. Dickson

Worms

A single row of trees planted when I was a child
Lombardi Poplars were much taller than I.
Father with his spade, tossed
shovels full of dirt as he dug 12 holes.
Crawling up close to one deep pit
I saw worms exposed from hiding places
below and I gently collected them
lined up next to me in rows, squirming.
The 12 Poplars stood as if waiting in line,
leaves fluttering with bulbous roots wrapped
in burlap and tied with twine –

To my dismay my father took the worms
and they were returned to their earthen homes
I looked down at my red sneakers -
the white rubber soles streaked with grass stains;
clots of dark soil caked the treads as
I stood and tramped around the base of
each freshly planted tree as he seated them,
my contribution to my father's project.

Today those trees stand 40 feet tall,
like great monolithic pillars
but pliable and swaying gently.
I recall the time I knelt by young saplings
with grass-stained sneakers but mostly
I remember the rows of my collected worms.

Untumbled Gem

Ferris Wheel

Against the red-streaked sky of a late
summer sunset; the great arched wheel sits idle,
open-laddered rungs and seats that once swung,
sneakered feet hanging below hands gripping firmly,
white-knuckled on the safety bar.

I once rode atop the Ferris wheel with deafening music
filling my ears; the wheel stopped higher than trees,
I begged my brother not to rock the seat; and I screamed,
closed my eyes until we descended, my legs stuck
on blue vinyl in the heat wearing seersucker shorts.

Today I stand in the distance, the wheel long since retired,
chains rusting, the seats against the spindly frame.

Why was the wheel left behind, the relic just a reminder?
I hear creaking as metal scrapes in an afternoon breeze,
a symphony of the past playing in my head.

Hurricane Press: Life is a Roller Coaster Anthology 2014

Julie A. Dickson

Cuckoo Clock

Awake again, I looked up at the ceiling.
What had I heard?
My mother's cuckoo clock,
chirping out every hour, the
relentless wooden carved bird, tiny
yet noisily announcing passing time.

A single chirp on the half hour,
enough to bring me back to consciousness.
When twelve cuckoos had come and gone
and the chirps became fewer,
I found myself drifting back to sleep;

but on many sleepless nights
I crept from my bed, silently down the stairs
to strangle that cuckoo - - don't worry
I only stopped the clock and when those
mornings came, I looked sheepishly
at my toast while my mother remarked
that the cuckoo clock had stopped once again.

Kind of a Hurricane Press: Tic Toc Anthology 2014

Keep Writing [For Mr. Brooks 1970]

Sitting in the first row
among the shy girls in 9th grade English;
A new student in a new school, alone
without friends or even familiar faces
to draw from, my vast loneliness spoken
only in the solitude, penciled thoughtfully
into journals and on decorated notepads,
not meant to be read aloud or shared beyond
the pale blue and white-flowered wallpapered room
of a teenaged girl, destined to remain holed-up
in the safe haven, writing volumes.

The teacher bellows,
bringing me back to stark consciousness.
I study his face, hidden behind thick wire-rimmed
glasses
and beneath a wild, scraggly beard
that he seemed to stroke and scratch often
and noisily, shuffling around by his desk.
His rumpled shirt was of no concern,
while he read aloud from Salinger or Steinbeck,
coercing the captive audience of apathetic students,
legs forced between the hard chairs and
connected desks made for smaller bodies;
covered with scratches, my fingers follow in
grooves,
the etched words of boredom,
the ghostly scratchings from past students I never
met.

I never bought into the rudeness,
of remarks spoken in whispers
from the back row of the classroom,
would never thought of sleeping,
chair leaning against the wall, threatening to fall

Julie A. Dickson

except for the foot held precariously on the chair in
front of him.

But, when the teacher's shoe came off;
flew madly through the air hitting the wall,
jolting the sleeping student awake,
many laughed.

During the whispered remarks, thrown shoe
and recitations of Milne and Poe,
I gained the courage to share.
This strangely bearded man in my new school,
this lover of books and writing would listen closely,
head cocked with unbelievable patience,
as young writers read their stories and poems
with trembling voices and shaking hands.
With his thoughtful encouragement,
with all those simple actions,
he gave a girl of 14 the will to keep writing.

The Poet's Touchstone 2013
The Harvard Press 2015

The Pink Fabric Clown

I first saw the pink fabric clown
from where I was perched on a window sill
in my hospital room, against the wishes
of attending nurses and my mother.
The pink fabric clown was held by
my grandmother, her brilliant white hair
shiny with *Aqua Net* as she stood in
the parking lot with my father and brother.
In disbelief, my eyes traveled to the
strange clown doll in her hand and
to my brother who held a red fabric clown,
twin to the pink in all other ways.

Grandmother waved as she handed
the pink fabric clown to my father, and
he made his way upstairs to my room.
 I already hated the pink fabric clown,
who was blameless but somehow became
the scapegoat for my anger. At age 7
I had fallen victim to mono, and my
beloved brown stuffed dog was taken,
an unsuspecting casualty, callously
tossed into a trash bin in the garage.

Stuffed dogs couldn't be washed --
germs, my mother explained as I grieved.

I dreamed of brown dog's sad demise
while holding the pink fabric clown
In a choke-hold, as if responsibility
lay in the flat plastic face with painted eyes
or the arms and legs of quilted fabric;
and somewhere within my sleep I flung
the innocent pink fabric clown
to the cold tile floor.

The Poet's Touchstone 2014

Julie A. Dickson

Pedaling

Careening down the road
my hair whips back in the wind,
I smile broadly,
tears almost blind my eyes.

Moments before, a struggle
as my red-sneakered feet
kept slipping off the pedals
before finally grabbing tread.

The handlebars jerked right and left,
hands sore from the tight grasp.
My father's hand pushed against
the back of my blue Schwinn seat

Pedaling like mad, I propelled
myself forward and he let go.
Terrified at first, the bike weaving wildly,
I felt out of control.

Tears almost blind my eyes,
I smile broadly,
my hair whips back in the wind
careening down the road.

Bony Knees

Looking down at two bony knees,
like hewn branches stripped clean,
appearing white and stark below
the hem of a red and navy blue plaid
Bobbie Brooks pleated skirt with
the gold-tone skirt pin I fidgeted with.

This skirt, coordinated with blouse and vest
matched navy blue knee socks I constantly
hiked back up over shapeless calves that
seemed to belong to someone else.

Specifically, the stiffly starched
and pressed clothing matched the
hard-creased demeanor of my
thin-lipped mother, her white lined mouth
issued disapproval - cast over my
disheveled appearance, shadowing
whatever preadolescent state of mind
I may have exhibited.

My face turned sour
in a saddened, slouched stance
with haunted eyes that looked down
at bony knees which might have been
encased in tights or hose, if my mother
had allowed such a fashion overhaul.

Julie A. Dickson

Instead, those two bony knees,
protrusions with terrifying white clarity
seemed to personify or describe,
the strangeness I begged to escape.

Oblivious to the changing times,
she sought to trap my adolescence
behind a well-built retaining wall,
adamantly resisting my emergence
into the unknown realm of womanhood;

as if the purposeful absence of nylon
covering those childish bony knees
could somehow postpone or prevent
her fear, my inevitable coming of age.

But the effect of those bony knees
emerging from red and blue wool plaid
was as odd as weather-bleached wood
against a landscape of colorful foliage,
those bony knees past the hem of my skirt.

The Almost Baseball Star

Maybe he thought he would excel
At being a great baseball star
He knew he could have hit the ball
Sending it almost up to Mars

The well-worn glove smelled leathery
Fit his small boyish hand so well
When standing outfield in his stance
Mesmerized, like under a spell

When time arrived to make his move;
His father sent him off to school
There was no chance for him to prove
Himself, his dad had raised no fool

"No son of mine will fail in life,
Now you will have to learn a trade"
Along with him agreed his wife,
"Successful men are all self-made"

"Play ball for fun" his dad chided
As disappointed son looked on;
To his brother, he confided
'bout future games he could have won

Today, the almost-baseball star
Stands gazing at the baseball field
Remembered the lost dream so far
In his past, he was force to yield

Julie A. Dickson

Dark Blue Purse

When my grandmother came to call,
her white-gloved hands grasping
A dark blue purse held closed
by a fine silver clasp,
She sat primly in a straight backed chair
with ankles so close together
as if tied with my father's twine.

The purse was sitting in her lap
nestled on her suit of herringbone;
my eyes followed strands of
stitching along its sides until
they disappeared under
the curved leather edge.
While adults sipped sweet tea
and talked of life –

my child's eyes were drawn
to the dark blue purse,
longing for the silver clasp to open,
to peer inside, emitting
the fragrance of my grandmother,

her lace handkerchief misted
lightly with lavender,
its odor wafting silently up
causing my eyes to close,
the aroma seeping slowly
into my sinuses -
breathing in the nectar.
Others may have wished
the tightly closed purse to open
for their own reasons;
but I longed for the fragrance of her,
the lavender depths of the dark blue purse

His First Goal

When my younger brother played
hockey, suited up in protective pads.
I often sat on a hard bench with frozen toes,
mesmerized by the spray of ice
that flew across the rink, like a blizzard,
briefly obscuring my view.

I was reminded of snowy fortresses we built
as kids. We denied the cold, stayed
outdoors for hours, shovels hollowed
out caves to sit in, our voices muffled.

No helmets on their fragile heads,
players' hair flying, eyes watering brightly
while the coal-black puck sailed across the ice.
I stood and cheered for him as he
scored his first goal and looked up at me.

My mittened hands clapped together;
I smiled at the bulky form of my brother,
Imagined his poster at home, his idol
number four silently approved.

Julie A. Dickson

September on Lake Ontario

Calm today, sun warm -
waves lapped at rocks in quiet rhythm.
I hear the call of a lone goose,
Canadian black markings clear
as it swims lazily –
far away from the chattering flock,
as if to say, "I need a few minutes".

Perhaps he is like me. I sit on a rough-hewn
boulder that edges the grassy outcropping
where the old public pier once stood.

Looking east to the row of cottages,
with open shutters, the dormered windows
trained on a blue expanse. All eyes on the
Great Lake, watching – past the calm blue.

I remember days when white-capped
thunderous waves crashed against the break walls,
toppling boats, eroding the shore, but not today.

Avocet Journal of Nature Poetry 2014

Red Sneakers

The dark green water
looked wild and angry;
chill of the water instantly
chased away the heat of day.

I stood on a lake pier near
the cottage with waves crashing
around me - the weeds that
attached themselves to rocks
look flattened, each wave
parting the strands like hair.

The red rocks, slippery and
weed-covered created
slimy steps into the lake.

My red sneakers were soaked
and squeaking; I clung to the
metal railing, feeling my feet
slide – even those red sneakers
didn't take hold, as if nothing was
meant to remain on those rocks.

Julie A. Dickson

Watermelon Pickles and Records for the Blind

The ticking of a hand-wound clock and the voice
of my father's aunt was what I first noticed
while sitting quietly in a Victorian chair with
curved wooden legs and needlepoint padded
seat, not really soft enough, nor was I able to sit
quietly for long. "Go into the kitchen and get
a watermelon pickle", his Aunt said merrily.

Of course, I'd had pickles – kosher dill, sweet
gherkins and homemade bread and butter
[though I couldn't understand what pickles
had to do with bread]
I looked at my mother's face, and she nodded
her permission for the kitchen excursion – I rose,
following my brother to the counter where the jar
sat. We exchanged skeptical glances and wondered
about the pale green spears in the canning jar.

Unconvinced that anything known as a watermelon
pickle would taste good, though the fruit of the
melon was a favorite of mine; I allowed my
brother to open the lid and waited to see his face
when he crunched.

Untumbled Gem

Back in the parlor, our aunt demonstrated her new
device, a record player and special disks
with braille labels, books and music, from the
Association for the Blind.
Her fingers nimbly removed one from paper jacket,
and soon the big band sounds of
Dorsey serenaded us.

With watermelon pickle in hand,
still uneaten, though
my brother appeared to survive his taste-test; I
watched my aunt's face come alive with the music.
Closing my eyes, I wondered about a world of
darkness with only sounds and quickly
opened them again, taking a bite of the pickle.

Julie A. Dickson

Wolf in Sheep's Clothing

He was such a smooth talker
Had a way with clever words
At the time I was enamored
In retrospect, it sounds absurd

Blue eyes like oceans, and his danced
I fell for his smile and warm demeanor
But once I was drawn into his web
I discovered he was a schemer

No advice cut through love's blind eye
My mother's words I was loathing
Little did I realize that my love
Was just a wolf in sheep's clothing

Vicariously

Living just outside the law
You were always the rebel
The careless risk-taker
Dangerous enough for us both

Never the outlaw, I was complacent
Sedate and boring in my quietude
What made me the fearful one?
My Libran sign of balance?
Avoiding anger and conflict at all costs?
Even to the point of denying myself,
Squelching my adventurous spirit

Watching you take risks from afar,
Braving the law and an upraised hand,
Caught in our father's cross-hairs
While I maintained invisibility

A flashing red streak- your first car
Speeding down the road scared me!
But I envisioned my hair blowing,
Top down, sitting in the passenger seat
In my dreams only- since I was a coward,
Never risking the flashing blues
But fearing more our father's wrath

I remained the responsible one,
In solitude, living vicariously
Through adventuresome characters
In books, while you played the outlaw

The Harvard Press 2016

Julie A. Dickson

Silent Now

Murmured voices and laughter
in soft tones seem to cascade,
washing over me like time,
enveloping my senses with reminders
of warm rolls dripping with jam;
or a hand-quilted blanket lain
gently over me by my mother's hand.

She is silent now, gone.

I recall caring glances and stories told,
well-planned meals on her stove.
Her black curls fell into waves,
dark mahogany hair rebelled,
escaping pins to curve against
her white neck and slender jaw.

She chose soft colors- rose and blue,
wrapped in silk and cotton,
the swish of her like musical notes.

I miss the sound, but hold the
camouflaged memories of her

Black Velvet Sky

Pin pricks of light I see above;
the stars hold many sparkling souls.
Inside my head an echo calls names
I knew in the past - they are gone now.

Great-Grandmother who was a seer -
she predicted tragedy and found items lost.
My grandfather must be a close by star;
when I close my eyes I see him smile
driving in his large black car.

Did I see the wink of an eye?
Perhaps the jovial grin of a great uncle
who told us his tales of asparagus…

What if when we die, our spirits join together,
a reunion of souls in the black velvet sky?
Each dot of brightness- a transient shining star
of every being who once lived.

Sparks of light watching over the rest of us,
waiting for their turn to be called upon -
a soul on its way to become a new life,
as far below we remember them.

Avocet Journal of Nature Poetry 2014

Julie A. Dickson

Yellowed Gloves

A pair of aged yellowed gloves
hastily placed into a drawer
beckon to me as I explore,
wander through my mother's house.

An eerie sensation creeps over me
when I think of her wearing gloves
and a black netted pill box hat,
fashions that I somehow evaded.

I fall back in clumsy, jerky steps
as my eyes flick over a portrait of her
hanging silently – but in my head
I seem to hear her soft rattling voice.

I think of my past journal entries
with pages erased and rewritten,
trying to capture some moment gone,
words thready and empty at best.

The Poet's Touchstone 2015

Cicada's Song
Based on Aesop's Fable: The Ant and the Grasshopper [aka Cicada]

Cicada sang his constant tune
while nearby worker ants collected.
Opinion was that he neglected
winter stores, instead he crooned.

Cicada's singing filled the air;
below ground nests were slowly filled.
Ants toiled, not one crumb was spilled;
Cicada continued without a care.

When snow covered the ground and trees,
ants nestled below with winter store,
Cicada's feeble attempt to ask for
food, denied despite his pleas.

Solemnly Cicada admitted
his song was meant to entertain.
They never told him to refrain;
this justification was submitted.

The colony felt collective anguish,
all summer Cicada's symphony
in fact, eased their litany - ants
agreed to aid him, not to banish.

Then all were feasting, no one perished.
in summer, the ants would work along
with Cicada nearby, sharing his song -
at winter feast, the music cherished.

Julie A. Dickson

Parchment

You look upon a blank pale canvas,
parchment or bleached white paper;
It beckons your communication
as though the process of applying ink
will somehow make the page heavier

If this writing becomes a story
or a metered poem with rhyme,
its very countenance will call to you,
commanding your sight to the page

Henceforth the ink will be as nectar,
nourishing your dry parched mouth.
The blank white page will summon
the vehicle, your pen to touch paper again

The Poet's Touchstone 2015

The Way that I find Peace

On the ground, my steps resound
I know that I am earth-bound
Alone the loneliness surrounds
Decisions made without a sound

What is the question, any suggestion?

Confusion mars my complex thoughts
Understanding, the truth is naught
Recalling the lessons I've been taught
Compared illusions, emotions wrought

How can I experiment? I find that I lament...

Above my head the perfect V
Sailing birds that know they're free
Would that I could fly with them,
Would I know eternity?

What is the answer, do I really matter?

Can I flee from the darkest space?
Would I be gone without a trace?
The cliffs that call, the rocks below
The V recedes, they'd never know

Creativity pacifies, I suddenly realize...
Writing has been my only release,
the way that I find peace

Julie A. Dickson

Wonderland

It's hard to think of winter

as a wonderland when your car is buried

beneath a foot of snow.

Shoveling can't be hurried -

just step back inside,

brew another pot of tea,

settle into an easy chair;

discover quiet tranquility.

Winter almost forgotten

wake to early morning dawn.

Sun shines onto drifts of white.

Silence is all you hear

seen through newly felt calm.

Snow un-melted overnight;

Now the wonderland is clear.

Portsmouth Herald: Random Acts of Poetry 2014

Avocet Journal of Nature Poetry 2016

Trees Wait

Inside the window
the cold is unnoticed,
the trees in winter
chilling air surrounding branches,
ice clinging,
glistening in sunlight,
wait patiently for spring.

Trees do not despair
as we do -
in the coldness and the snow.
We are the ones who cannot abide the cold,
Trees wait in silence,
branches bend
and sometimes break,
but they do not cry as we do,
when icy fingers touch our souls.

Julie A. Dickson

Winter Window

At first the glass is clear

During the cold black night

Not even a cloud in sight

A drop in temperature

Crystal forms a faint design

Suddenly I feel inclined

To don an extra sweater

At the window, crystal expanded

Interlocked lace, more than imagined

Where once the glass was clear

Has become a crystalized fantasy

Obscuring my view of reality

Against the Storm [Triolet]

Shuttered windows against the storm

Birds huddled high up in the trees

Sit by the firelight that's warm

Shuttered windows against the storm

For sunbathed afternoons I mourn

Comforter wrapped around my knees

Shuttered windows against the storm

Birds huddled high up in the trees

Julie A. Dickson

I'm Warm

I'm not cold

and if I may be so bold

as to remark that in deepest dark

I'm still not cold

One might surmise

that my temperature rise

Is due to my age but let me dissuade

though I know it implies…

Really, I'm warm

yes, despite a snow storm

on a winter's night my thermometer's right

I'm inclined to inform

Please have no worry

if you feel you must scurry

to nearer the fire –

I'd be apt to perspire, or

to dash outdoors in a hurry!

New Grange

To stand before an ancient mound
on the Irish countryside,
stones hewn and balanced,
silent structure stands sentinel,
cavern in deep darkness -
but for the winter solstice, waiting
for early morning light to
Illuminate the ritual alter.

If I almost close my eyes
I can imagine the Druid priests
rowing across deep blue water,
walking on rough paths
to the sacred mound
as the early morning light enters.
I stood where they stood once
awaiting their illumination.

From Thor

How fair the blackened, starless sky,
it waits, impending, watchful nox,
broken, cut of lightning bolt as
Thor's saber severs, silence halts
dusky shadows with mighty flash;
shuddering presence rumbles back
Thunder-giant's hammer drops down
to startled ground, awaits response.

Reverberating, tree roots shake,
meek rodents roused from deepest dreams,
in burrows, while large boulders slip
from steadfast hill, the rocks dislodged,
breaking roots down steep rolling path,
the synchronized descent toward ground
unobstructed echoes pounding,
tenacious force disrupts the night.

Ah, raindrops, misty morning breaks;
dew-covered leaves dispel minute
iridescent droplets, descend
to beckoning dry grasses - are
stretching up as dancing lasses
for nourishment, for nature's drink;
wisdom echoes eternal laugh
from Thor, from whence the thunder rolled.

Of No Means

Dejected gentleman of no means
loosened tie it seems, on starched collar,
shoulders a bit slumped in his despair.

Reject from opportunity, dumped -
was educated with care, he was
meticulous in his demeanor
and subjugated by industry,
loved history; chose economics -
it was still perversely ironic.

He thought himself bright, bold and clever
yet skills overqualified now for
applied jobs, even mediocre
would resolve to accept even this
desperate measure to merely survive -
not thrive as once accomplished job meant
to him – hustling in daily routine,
now in extremely low self-esteem.

Recalls the former good life he viewed
then as persevering daily strife -
he would humbly, gratefully return
to accepted recognized mundane.

He certainly would vow to function
and honestly promise to refrain
from eyes cast over nearby fences
where abundantly green grasses fade
to yellow-gold and even to brown.

A frown crosses the face of a lost
dejected gentleman of no means.

Julie A. Dickson

The Stranger

He was a man that no one loved
yet he cared about everyone he met
magnanimous, giving all he had --
remained anonymous as he was clad
in threadbare clothing, taken for homeless
yet selfless, keeping almost nothing.
He wandered the streets offering
assistance to humans and animals
yet ignored as the public feared him.

When he passed away alone one night
no one wondered who he had been,
or pondered the deeds he had performed.
They buried him without ceremony.
If only someone had recognized
the kindness of his loving heart, but
instead perceived truth and blindness
obscured their scornful visions of a stranger.
He was never any danger to anyone.

Are Those My Hands?

I look down at the lines on my once smooth and
rugged hands
not recognizing them as I button my shirt with effort.

Is that my hair?
I look in the mirror at the once dark hair that is now
threaded
with strands of silver more so than the brown I
remember.

Are those my eyes?
Behind thick lenses that I must wear to read or to drive
I recall such keen vision, reading signs from a
distance.

Can I hear the music?
I touch my ears and wonder if I am catching all that is
said,
I recall years of wonderful music and conversation.

Is that my voice?
I hear myself greet friends and strangers with
shakiness
or a slight tremble in the words I speak.

Are these my legs?
Holding onto cane or banister, the light-footed pace of
youth
replaced by this slow gait of uncertainty

Do I have memories?
I remember times of hardship and times of luck
So many years behind, but how many still ahead?

Are those my hands?

The Harvard Press 2012

Julie A. Dickson

Back When I was Old

Sometimes I recall when I was old,
when my legs betrayed my will to run;
I cautiously ambled from room to room,
making slow progress past claw-footed chairs,
and a couch with gaudy flowers and big pillows.

Now my chair is wheeled down long tiled hallways,
passing people I don't know
or, have I forgotten them?
They say I am dying, and I don't speak to anyone;
I sit still for hours. When I close my eyes,
I see my mother;
and it seems lovely to gaze upon her face again.

Back when I was old, my TV at home stayed on,
the recliner curved around my form like a friend.
They called me Grampy, and when family visited,
we spoke of books, raking leaves, and the bright
yellow convertible Volkswagen Beetle I could no
longer drive.

Now I play games like a child; we toss balls
and sing;
My days are filled with oatmeal, singing
and creamed spinach.
I stare at my food tray, wondering if I ever
played ball
or liked creamed spinach back when I was old.

Portsmouth Herald: Spotlight - Poems from the Hoot 2014

Hand-in-Hand

The outline of an older man

shadows across a chalky sidewalk.

A young boy stands atop the shadow,

looking up, his small fingers clasped firmly

but softly held in the age-mottled hand

of his white-haired grandfather.

They cross the street hand-in-hand

on their special weekly excursion,

the boy brightening when approaching

their favorite ice cream shop.

Grandfather always orders a Spanish sundae,

enjoying each salty red-skinned peanut;

in contrast to the boy's pink-hued strawberry
shortcake,

whipped cream and a cherry, saved until the last.

The boy savors each bite in the shadow of an older
man.

Five Willows Literary Review 2015

Julie A. Dickson

Old Fiddler

Trouble strumming
fingers cold in the morning
used to play easily;
Arthritis came without warning.
Crippled hands curl
round my bow, slowly move,
lucky- songs I know well,
hands slip into a groove.

Elders Serve Us Well [for Pat Parnell]

Elders revered in the ancient cultures
Worshipped as wise and sought for their knowledge
Silver locks marked as a passage of time
Thoughtful demeanor behind their disguise

Wise men and crones often shared advice
Societies changed, cultures were altered
Leaders set previous icons aside
Perceived as knowing while the world faltered

Articulate artists, poets convene
Boisterous banters, pedantic words swell
We understand with a unison nod
With life's wisdom, our elders serve us well

The Poet's Touchstone 2014
The Harvard Press 2014

Julie A. Dickson

Rusted Hinges and Coarse Bread

Heavy coal black wrought iron-gate
Stood sentinel at the entry
Rusted hinges in need of oil
But did not cause its strength to wane

The man's back was strong and rippled with
Muscles, not built for show – the logs
He moved from truck to conveyor
His arms heaved wood as the belt turned

The old mare whinnied softly, her
Bay coat and mane grown thin with age
She ambled across the pasture
Legs knobby with arthritis now

The woman stood at the stove cutting meat
For stew, gnarled hand pushed the knife
To the hardwood block, worn with cuts
Not noticing her back was aching

His weathered hand found the soft towel
Left for him by the pump-house well
She laid the bowls on the table
He carried the basket of bread

They sat wordlessly in their chairs
Dipping the coarse bread into stew
Eyes met as the daylight faded
The glances they shared spoke silently

The Harvard Press 2013

Tomorrow at Dawn

Contemplating consciously
mayhem and confusion;
what you remember happening
may just be an illusion

Forgotten misfortunes
may not be what they seem;
now you must stay focused
your thoughts upon a dream

Left behind the chaos
emerging yet unscathed;
remember all the voices
and all the plans you made

Now is your forever,
dreams in silence dwell,
at a quiet hilltop
in a shady knoll

Remember words that saved you;
when did time get lost?
Forever sealed your memories,
to the seas are tossed

Julie A. Dickson

The Sea Will Call

Sons of the fathers, taken to sea
Though some will follow, landlubbers will flee
A fisherman's life is not meant for all
But for the true sailor, the sea - she will call

Wayfarers' voices adrift on the waves
As darkness is falling, they cannot be saved
Scurry on ship deck, pull ropes, secure boom
The fishin's been hearty; it makes the gulls croon.

Sons of the fathers, taken to sea
Though some will follow, landlubbers will flee
A fisherman's life is not meant for all
But for the true sailor, the sea - she will call

By day the fishermen cast out their lines
when night approaches, they shan't be entwined
at sea in night shadows, men have been lost
Rocky coast beckons, on reef they'd be tossed

Sons of the fathers, taken to sea
Though some will follow, landlubbers will flee
A fisherman's life is not meant for all
But for the true sailor, the sea - she will call

Holds over-heavy, fish laden their hull
Hands waved in presence of lone eager gull
Bountiful take from the cold azure sea
Sky streaked in ruby as night makes its plea

Sons of the fathers, taken to sea
Though some will follow, landlubbers will flee
A fisherman's life is not meant for all
But for the true sailor, the sea - she will call

Untumbled Gem

Homeward the sailors to pub and cold ale
Drink up tonight lads, tomorrow we sail!
Fish market booming with catch of the day
Celebrate full nets of fish - fiddler's sway

Sons of the fathers, taken to sea
Though some will follow, landlubbers will flee
A fisherman's life is not meant for all
But for the true sailor, the sea - she will call

Tune of the ocean, the tide's jaunty dance
On the sea's bounty, they all take a chance
Families depending on weathered da's face
Love of the salt air, they just can't erase

Sons of the fathers, taken to sea
Though some will follow, landlubbers will flee
A fisherman's life is not meant for all
But for the true sailor, the sea - she will call

Page & Spine 2013

Revised 2014- with Dan Miner

Julie A. Dickson

Crimson Sails

Windswept hair
Blown away from her face
Years etched into lines,
Creases of laughter and sorrow

Willow branches sway
Back from rocky cliff
Exposing hairline crevasses
Into which sand collects

She walks along the coast
Dress billows in filmy puffs
Filled with light and air
Much like the clouds above

Ripples swirl and ebb
Behind the keel, rudder turned
Slightly, her sails expanded
Carrying the vessel through current

She sits upon a rocky cliff
Willow branches rustling
Gold burnished hair swept back
As sunset shines on crimson sails

Avocet Journal of Nature Poetry 2015

Within My Reach

Warm morning sun that shines upon my face
When walking by the sea, as terns prevail.
The echoes of the birds, it can't erase
I glance at passing boat with crimson sail.

White-tipped cold ocean waves leap up in crests;
Sun kissed, the sparkling fish swim up toward light.
The gulls that glide appear to never rest,
I hope to see a dolphin rise in flight

The sand beneath my feet adheres to skin;
I gather shells and pebbles cast ashore.
I search my soul, recall the thoughts within,
Release the silent echoes from my core

Refreshed, I walk the early morning beach
The peace I seek is there within my reach

Avocet Journal of Nature Poetry 2015

Julie A. Dickson

Waves

The sun reflects on water
the sky is full of birds
I watch the sea in wonder
and listen to what I've heard

Look out to the ocean
when the sea is calm
The waves are barely moving
the sun is like a song

When you feel the warm breeze
and the waves fall away
The sands reach out around you
as peaceful as the day

Low Tide

The view this afternoon is peaceful
With large expanse of blue stretching out
Rocky shore uninhabited

Today I see a veritable water highway:
A freighter plodding slowly, billowing smoke
Sails moving leisurely, crisscrossing lanes
With an occasional motorboat hurrying between
them

A small trawler is adrift with *Miss Molly* on her stern
Fishing poles upright from top beam - lines taut
Thin as etched pencil marks disappearing into the
water
Miss Molly pitches in rhythm with the gentle waves

Bent over beachcombers with brightly colored pails
Collect iridescent shells and muted sea glass
A lone sunbather, legs shiny with oil
Sits atop the highest rock

Its low tide and the pools between the rocks
Are teaming with stranded fish – mouths opening
In search of the water that splashes only teasingly
Delaying the return to preferred submergence

Five Willows Literary Review 2015
Poetry Quarterly 2015

Julie A. Dickson

Walk with Me

Down by the dunes
Where the sand is warm
And all the sounds
Capture thoughts and more

I'm sitting alone
As the waves flow in,
Leaving their treasures
On the sandy shore

Walk with me
And feel the warm breeze
That cause
The grasses to bend

So peacefully,
In silent dreams
I walk with you,
Beside my friend

Julie A. Dickson

About the Author: Julie A. Dickson

Member:
Poetry Society of NH
Writers in the Round
Pen Click Poets ,/

Publications:
Five Willows Literary Review
The Avocet Journal of Nature Poetry
The Portsmouth Herald
The Harvard Press
Smoky Quartz
Page & Spine
Van Gogh's Ear
Poetry Quarterly
The Poet's Touchstone

Other books by Julie A. Dickson

Prey Tell [poetry editor] 2015
 Available only through Owl Moon Raptor Center

Bullied into Silence 2014 Piscataqua Press
Drawing him Out 2013
The Last Wish [children's] 2013
*Fat Cat Meets Bonnie [children's] 2013
*Tails of Rescue [non fiction] 2012
*The Seven Trials of Kiera Snow 2012
*The Tree House Mysteries 2012
*The Nine Lives of Here Kitty 2012
*Girl from the Shadows 2011
*Chronicles of Dragon Lore 2005
Fat Cat Buys a Hat [children's] 2005
Caterpillar [children's] 2005
Forest Nectars [poetry] 1997 Morriss Publishing

*Available on Amazon

Untumbled Gem